The Buddha Smiles

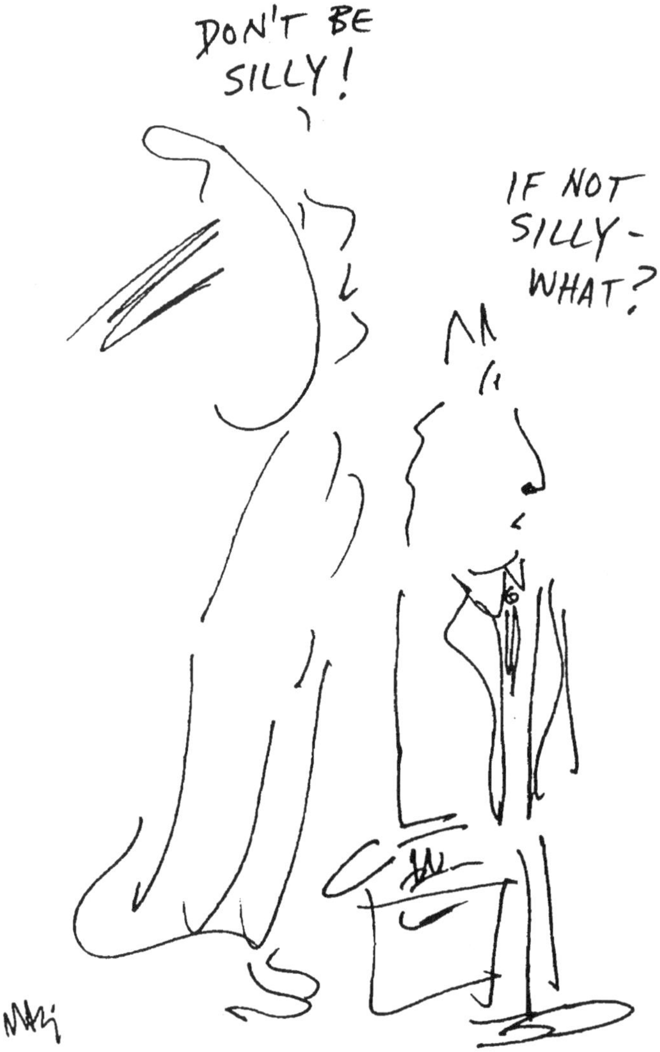
DON'T BE SILLY!
IF NOT SILLY - WHAT?

The Buddha Smiles

A Collection of Dharmatoons

Mari Gayatri Stein

With Contributions by
Sylvia Boorstein
Sharon Salzberg
and Joseph Goldstein

WHITE CLOUD PRESS
Ashland, Oregon

02 01 00 99   5 4 3 2 1

Cover Design by David Rupee, Impact Publications, Medford, Oregon
Cover Art by Mari Gayatri Stein
Printed in Canada

Library of Congress Cataloging-in-Publication Data

Stein, Mari, 1947-
   The Buddha smiles : A collection of Dharmatoons / Mari Gayatri
Stein ; with contributions by Sylvia Boorstein, Sharon Salzberg, and
Joseph Goldstein.
      p.   cm.
   ISBN 1-883991-28-5
   1. Buddhism Caricatures and Cartoons. 2. Dharma (Buddhism)-
Humor. 3. Meditation--Humor.   I. Boorstein, Sylvia. II. Salzberg,
Sharon. III. Goldstein, Joseph, 1944-   . IV. Title.
BQ4060.S74 1999
294.3'02'07--dc21   99-27751
                                                          CIP

TABLE OF CONTENTS

Foreword by Sylvia Boorstein   vi
Humor and Buddhism by Joseph Goldstein   viii
Meditation and Humor by Sharon Salzberg   xi

1. The First Three Noble Truths: The Existence of
   Suffering; The Origin of Suffering; The End of Suffering   1
2. The Fourth Noble Truth: The Noble Eightfold Path,
   The Path to the End of Suffering   23
3. The Spiritual Powers and The Precepts   61
4. The Hindrances   97
5. Vipassana: The Practice of Insight into Our True Nature   141
6. Metta   175

Notes   221
Glossary   222

Foreword
By Sylvia Boorstein

DISCOVERING THAT THE MIND, uncomplicated by confusion and passion, is benevolent and gracious and compassionate and generous is a great joy. Perhaps the greatest of joys. How strange it is, then poignant, really that while happiness is natural, we sometimes need to work so hard to find it.

Throughout history, all the great spiritual traditions have included the way of the contemplative — the meditative path — as one of the routes to realization. In the West, in our times, many people use the model of the mind that the Buddha taught 2500 years ago and the Buddha's instructions to "See for yourself if it's true" to inform their meditation practice. Thousands of students have practiced using the techniques of mindfulness cultivated in the context of stillness and silence. They go on retreats. What they are hoping is that they will experience directly and personally what the Buddha taught as Dharma — the truth of how things really are. And they are trusting that seeing that truth clearly is the key to genuine happiness. It's a well placed trust.

The retreat form of practice is odd in a Western context where monasticism has been reserved for clergy and required lifelong commitment. Meditators at mindfulness retreats become celibate, silent monastics for a weekend, or a week, or a month, and then move back into their relational lives with whatever insight has been part of their experience. Often they return for more retreat periods, and find the form familiar and the slow pace and simple schedule supportive and sustaining. First-timers often find it funny.

Mari sees and hears with a cartoonist's wit. At her first mindfulness retreat I said to the group, as the opening sentence of a Dharma talk on the Hindrances, "I wish I knew a cartoonist who could draw five meditators — lay people just like us — all sitting with their eyes closed, identical calm visage. Then I'd like the artist to draw a big balloon over the head of each meditator with little bubbles trailing from each balloon to each head signifying, 'This is what's in this mind.' One balloon would have an ice cream cone, or a Hawaiian beach; another would have a war, or @!!??XX*!!; another would be filled with clouds or fog; another with an erupting volcano; one with ???. Then I could teach about Lust and Aversion and Torpor and Restlessness and Doubt. But I'd need a sequence of drawings. Each one would have the same people, same inscrutable visages, same balloons. But the balloons would change places. Then I could teach that every experience passes, and that *all* the Hindrance energies are part of everyone's experience."

An hour later Mari's drawing was on the bulletin board. Her drawing had seven meditators. The seventh meditator's balloon was empty. And Mari's drawing had a dog. His balloon had a bone in it.

That's Mari. She is very funny. Her cartoonist's eye view is balanced by good understanding. She says, with a few strokes of her pen, what would take many words to explain *and* she makes us laugh. May the delight that arises in our hearts as we meet her images of us coming and going inspire our practice for the benefit of all beings.

Humor & Buddhism[§]
by Joseph Goldstein

A SENSE OF HUMOR is indispensable in the practice of the Dharma, both on retreat and on the roller coaster of our life in the world. When we reflect for a moment on the quality of mind a sense of humor implies, we see that it creates some inner space. Being able to see the humor, the lightness, and the emptiness of phenomena is really a great blessing during those times when we become caught in the various dramas of our lives.

The Buddhist texts provide a whole explanation of manifestations of humor. They do it, of course, in the traditionally dry fashion of the Abhidharma, the Buddhist psychology. The texts describe the different kinds of laughs people have at various stages along the path. When something strikes uncultured worldlings as being funny, they will roll about on the floor. One in middling stages of enlightenment will laugh out loud. Arhats, or fully enlightened beings, will laugh showing their teeth. And the Buddha simply smiled. The point is that there are refinements to the quality of humor.

Being with different teachers and seeing so many different styles of Dharma teachings and presentations has taught me much about humor, including understanding that humor is often quite a cultural matter. I have seen the most strict and demanding Asian teachers almost lose control laughing at a particular joke that does not seem funny at all from a Western point of view. At one time, the late Burmese master Venerable Taungpulu Sayadaw was giving a Dharma talk. He always lectured in the traditional fashion, holding a ceremonial fan in front of him. He was talking about mind and matter, and one of the yogis asked whether a dog has both. The Sayadaw could hardly stop laughing. He thought that was the funniest question as he reflected on what the alternative might be.

Humor also serves us in times of great difficulty or suffering. It helps create spaciousness of mind around the suffering and can help loosen the bonds of identification. One example of this is Oscar Wilde's probably apocryphal last words. He had been released from prison a sick, broken, impoverished, disgraced, and dying man. He went to Paris, where he died in a cheap rooming house in a slum.

The wallpaper in his rented room was horrendously ugly, and Wilde was nothing if not a stylish man. It is said that just before Wilde died, as he lay on his deathbed, he turned his face to the wall and said, "One of us has got to go."

[§] From Joseph Goldstein, *Insight Meditiation* (Boston, Shambhala Publications, 1993), pp. 163-164.

The Buddha Smiles

THE COMPLETE EXPERIENCE OF DOG

(MIND AND MATTER INCLUDED ~ NO BATTERIES REQUIRED)

The Buddha Smiles

~ x ~

Meditation and Humor

by Sharon Salzberg

MEDITATION, THOUGH WONDERFUL, can be hard work. As with most hard work, it's greatly benefited by a good dose of humor. Humor is a balm that can frequently soothe the painful edges we encounter in intensive self-awareness practice, whether it's on the meditation cushion or in the midst of daily life. It is often noted that naming our demons is a good first step toward dis-empowering their hold on us. If we reach a time when our response is to gently laugh at their appearance, then we can have a moment of more freedom.

Humor can activate the factor of joy, which is an opening toward enlightenment. An ordinary event, colored by humor, becomes delightful.

Many Dharma teachings are sprinkled with humor. In part this may be because they are offered by skilled public speakers or gifted teachers who know how to open us gently to what is true. And it may also be a result of the clear seeing and open hearts that are the fruits of practice. With a clear mind we can often notice the absurdity of the human predicament, and an open and loving heart infuses this perception with joy.

The Buddha Smiles

With gratitude to the teachings of the Dharma, Shinzen Young, Sylvia Boorstein, Sharon Salzberg, Joseph Goldstein, Ann Buck, and all those who contributed their wise words to *The Buddha Smiles*, as well as Steven Scholl, Robert, Suni, Patricia, Wolf, Cougar, Moon, Morgan, Moss, Mulph, and Muse.

And to my mom.

Chapter One
The First Three Noble Truths:
Suffering Exists / The Origin of Suffering / The End of Suffering

THE FIRST NOBLE TRUTH:
SUFFERING EXISTS

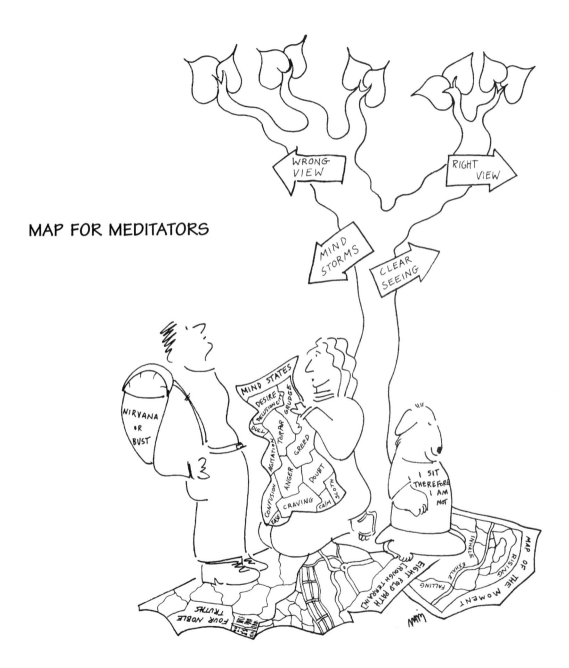

MAP FOR MEDITATORS

"Years and years of going to the left or right, going to yes or no, going to right or wrong, has never really changed anything. Scrambling for security has never brought anything but momentary joy. . . . We keep moving around seeking pleasure, seeking comfort, and the satisfaction that we get is very short-lived. . . . We desire our birthright which is the middle path, an open state of mind that can relax with paradox and ambiguity."[1]
Pema Chodron

LOOKING FOR MEANING

The Second Noble Truth:
The Origin of Suffering

THE UNQUENCHABLE MIND.

"You know the classic Zen vow: 'Desires are inexhaustible; I vow to put an end to them.' Well, you can't *want* to put an end to desire — that would be just another ego project. But you can begin to see that desire itself can be investigated: Practice is really an investigation into everything, not an effort to be a certain way — the main thing that holds practice back is the ambition to get somewhere. And we can persistently practice, not 'to get somewhere,' but with the one true desire that our practice benefit not just ourselves but all sentient beings."[2]
Charlotte Joko Beck

THE MIND IS A MUNCHING ANIMAL

I'M ATTACHED
, SO SUE ME.
ATTACHMENT QUIZ
are you attached to:
1. SENSE PLEASURES?
2. YOUR OPINIONS AND IDEAS?
3. RITES AND RITUALS EMPTY OF HEART?
4. THE IDEA OF A PERMANENT SELF THAT NEVER DIES?
total Your Score And Go on to The Next Meditation!!!!!
Moss

THE INSIGHT OF IMPERMANENCE

WOMAN IN SUN HAT LOOKING INTO THE EYES OF DEATH.

"Is it not incredible that
although we witness others
dying all around us, we continue
to believe that we alone shall not
come face-to-face with death?"
The Bhagavad-Gita

WE BEGIN OPENING UP TO WHAT IS PAINFUL;
THE TRUTH MAY BE HARD TO FACE BUT WILL NEVER HARM US.

LOOKING INTO THE EYES OF SOMEONE LOOKING INTO THE EYES OF DEATH.

"Fundamentally we are so completely alone that we are not even here to keep ourselves company."[3] Gil Fronsdal

"There is an enormous possibility of getting
side-tracked into self-conscious holiness,
of putting energy into acting the part
of a spiritual person." [4]
Sylvia Boorstein

THERE ARE SOME PECULIAR NOTIONS ABOUT
WHAT CONSTITUTES BEING SPIRITUAL. DON'T MISS THE MEANING FOR THE MALA.
DON'T PASS UP THE PATH FOR THE PROSTRATIONS.

WHAT IS TRUE LIES IN THE HEART.
DON'T BE FOOLED BY APPEARANCES.

WHEN YOU INSIST ON BEING RIGHT, OFTEN YOU ARE LEFT.

THE THIRD NOBLE TRUTH:
THE END OF SUFFERING

CHAPTER TWO
THE FOURTH NOBLE TRUTH:
THE NOBLE EIGHTFOLD PATH,
THE PATH TO THE END OF SUFFERING

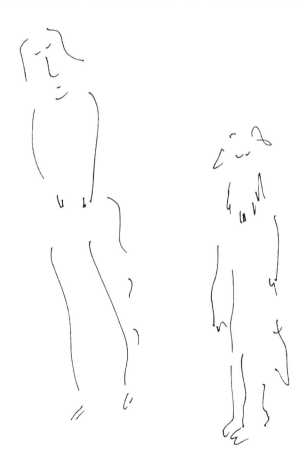

I THINK I'VE FOUND A SYSTEM AT LAST. R. UTSALEMA C.. THAT'S HOW I'LL REMEMBER.

Right understanding
Right thought
Right speech
Right action
Right livelihood
Right effort
Right mindfulness
(and)
Right concentration...

R.. UT.. SA.. LEM ...AC
R.. UTS.. A.. LEMAC
RUTS.. ALE.. MAC
RU.. TSAL..EM..AC..
R...

THEY SAY IT'S THE PATH THAT LEADS TO HAPPINESS, BUT IT APPEARS YOU'RE INTENT ON TAKING A DETOUR.

HUMAN BEINGS SURE KNOW HOW TO COMPLICATE LIFE. HOW ABOUT A NICE STROLL IN THE GARDEN?

NIRVANA 1
NIRVANA 2
NIRVANA 3

**THE STRIVING STUDENT
STRIKES AGAIN**

WOMAN WITH HER HAIR ON FIRE TAKES THE OPPORTUNITY
TO LIGHT HER CANDLE.

WHEN YOUR MIND
IS BURNING UP
WITH THINKING,
DON'T FEED
THE FIRE
WITH FRESH
THOUGHTS.

LET IT
BURN OUT
NATURALLY IN
YOUR MEDITATION.
DON'T SUPPRESS
IT EITHER,
OR IT MAY
SMOULDER FOR
A VERY
LONG TIME.

PAIN AND JOY WILL COME AND GO,
AND THE MIND WILL REMAIN ESSENTIALLY TRANQUIL.

Mari Gayatri Stein

EQUANIMITY IS THE ATTITUDE THAT MAKES YOU FEEL BETTER.
SO DO LOVE AND COMPASSION.

WHEN YOU'RE STUCK IN TAFFY
TAKE A BIG BITE

YUMMY IN MY TUMMY

EQUANIMITY HAS TWO COMPONENTS ~
LACK OF JUDGEMENT, BODY BEING RELAXED.

UNCOVERING THE JEWEL

when the sky is falling
use it as a blanket

TRANSMUTING OUR DIFFICULTIES INTO A LIBERATING FORCE.

A MEDITATOR IS SOMEONE WHO NEVER SCRATCHES UNTIL SHE OR HE HAS CLEARLY ITCHED. BE THE WAVE NOT A PARTICLE. THE WAVE FLOWS, MERGES, MELTS. A PARTICLE REMAINS SEPARATE AND IS RIGID. YOU CAN'T SCRATCH A WAVE.

BUT YOU CAN SCRATCH ME, SO GET BUSY.

IF WE ARE FULLY PRESENT IN THE MOMENT,
TIME WILL BE SUSPENDED.
THAT FEELING OF BEING TRAPPED OR OVERWHELMED
WILL EVAPORATE.

PRECISELY WATCH THE WAVE OF IMPERMANENCE ~
MOVEMENT IN THE BODY OR MOVEMENT IN THE MIND.
FOR ONE MOMENT WE CAN DO THIS.
STAY IN THE NOW.

THERE IS A WAY TO CAST OUR GAZE
FORWARD AND BACKWARD
AND STILL KEEP OUR ENERGY
PLANTED IN THE PRESENT
WITHOUT BEING UPROOTED.

"Diligence counts even when you are not clear about your intentions. When we bring the body to the cushion, when we sit, walk and keep silence, the mind takes care of itself. It actually tends in the direction of clarity. Vipassana and metta practices are similar in that they both help us to be alert and composed with non-grasping attention to current experience."[1]
Sylvia Boorstein

DILLIGENCE COUNTS

TIMES WILL BE EASY, OTHERS WILL BE DIFFICULT.
JUST BEGIN AGAIN. IT IS IMPORTANT TO PERSIST.

I'VE GOT THE FREEDOM EQUATION.
PAIN TIMES RESISTANCE
EQUALS SUFFERING —
NO RESISTANCE
NO SUFFERING,
YOU DO THE MATH.

EUREKA!
ANOTHER SCIENTIFIC
BREAKTHROUGH.

SO IF YOU STOP
RESISTING MY
REQUESTS FOR
SECOND HELPINGS,
IT WILL MEAN
THE END OF
YOUR SUFFERING.

"When a feeling is not allowed to move as it wishes through the volume of the body, that feeling if it is unpleasant is experienced as suffering, and if it is pleasant fails to give complete satisfaction. This is true whether the feeling is of physical or emotional origin. . . .

FULLY FREE AND FULLY FEELING.

. . . . If the feeling is experienced without congealing or resistance, that feeling, if it is pleasant will be completely fulfilling, and if it is unpleasant will feel more like a release and growth experience than an experience of suffering."[2] Shinzen Young

FEARLESSLY RIDING THE WAVES OF EXPERIENCE AND
LEAVING THE CLOUDS OF DELUSION IN YOUR WAKE.

WOMAN WHOSE FUNDAMENTAL NATURE MANIFESTS ITSELF
IN A MOMENT OF SIMPLE HAPPINESS.

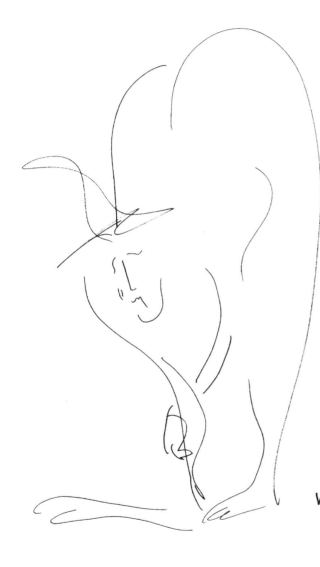

LEANING
INTO
THE MOUTH
OF GRIEF,
YOU LET
YOURSELF BE
SWALLOWED UP.

FREE OF RESISTANCE
AND FULL OF ACCEPTANCE,
WE CAN FEEL AND NOT LET
THE MIND CONGEAL.
WE REMAIN FREE
IN THE FACE OF
ALL EMOTIONS
WHEN THEY ARE FLUID.

TURNING DEPRESSION INTO AN EXPRESSION OF ENERGY.

WHEN YOU ARE CAUGHT IN EMOTION, ASK THE QUESTION:
ARE THE VOICES TRUE OR NOT? WILL I BE LOVED?

LETTING
YOUR
HEART
BREAK
OPEN.

"Cool loneliness allows us to look honestly and without aggression at our own minds. . . . We give it up and just look directly with compassion and humor at who we are. Then loneliness is no threat and heartache no punishment. . . . This is called the middle way, or the sacred path of the warrior. . . . Right there in the moment of sadness and longing, could you relax and touch the limitless space of the human heart?

"When we can rest in the middle, we begin to have a nonthreatening relationship with loneliness, a relaxing and cooling loneliness that completely turns our usual fearful patterns upside down. . . . There are six ways of describing this kind of cool loneliness. They are: less desire, contentment, avoiding unnecessary activity, complete discipline, not wandering in the world of desire and not seeking security from one's discursive thoughts." [3]
Pema Chodron

THE GARDEN OF DELIGHTS

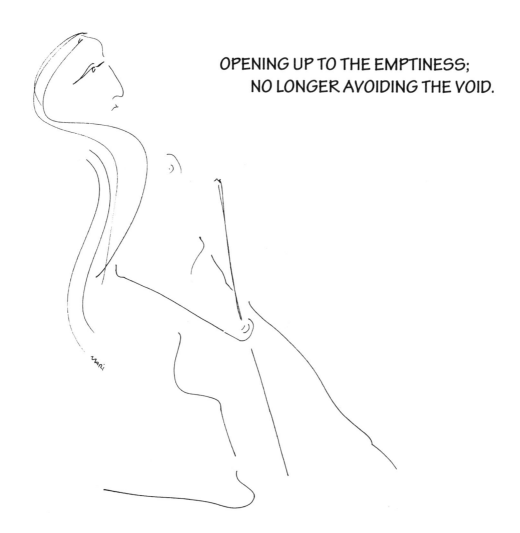

OPENING UP TO THE EMPTINESS;
NO LONGER AVOIDING THE VOID.

FALLING APART AND FALLING TOGETHER,
EXPLODING AND IMPLODING, RELAXING INTO THE STABILITY OF SPACE.

WHEN WE OPEN UP COMPLETELY TO PHYSICAL PAIN
BY ESCAPING INTO THE PAIN RATHER THAN RESISTING IT,
THE PAIN ACTUALLY BREAKS UP AND WE UNDERGO
A PHYSICAL PURIFICATION. THERE IS NO SUFFERING.

WHEN WE OPEN UP COMPLETELY TO EMOTIONAL PAIN,
LETTING OURSELVES DIE INTO THE FEELINGS
INSTEAD OF PUSHING THEM DOWN,
THE SENSE OF SEPARATION DISSOLVES
AND WE EXPERIENCE A PURIFICATION OF CONSCIOUSNESS
WHICH BRINGS FORTH OUR INTUITIVE WISDOM,
INSIGHT AND CLARITY. WE FEEL INTENSELY ALIVE.

EMOTION IS A TANGLING OF THOUGHT AND FEELING.
TEASE APART, DISCERN AND ISOLATE THE COMPONENTS
OF ANY ASPECT OF EXPERIENCE; AND THERE IS FREEDOM.

DIFFICULT EMOTIONS ARE LIKE A FEELING CREATURE
WITH ITS OWN LIFE FORCE.

DO YOU FIND
YOURSELF BECOMING
MEAN BECAUSE
YOU ARE STILL
BLAMING EVERYBODY
ELSE FOR NOT
DOING WHAT
YOU WANT
WITH YOUR LIFE?

WOMAN WHOSE ANGER HAS TAKEN ROOT
BECAUSE SHE'S STILL ATTACHED TO THE IDEA THAT LIFE IS FAIR.

ANTIDOTE TO ANGER:
COUNT TO TEN.
NOTE SENSATIONS IN THE BODY.
BREATHE.
TAKE TIME TO LET THE MUD IN YOUR MIND SETTLE.
CONSIDER THE EFFECT AND THE LONG TERM PRICE OF YOUR WORDS AND ACTIONS.
PUT YOURSELF IN THE OTHER DOG'S PAWS.
TAKE TIME TO WAG YOUR TAIL A LITTLE.

HOW DOES HE SMELL?

MY HUMAN HAS NO NOSE.

TERRIBLE. WOOF WOOF. NO SERIOUSLY FOLKS, HAVE YOU HEARD THE ONE ABOUT THE POODLE WHO HAD A CLOSE SHAVE WOOF WOOF.

ANECDOTE TO ANGER

MEDITATION SIPHONS OFF THE POOLS OF OLD COLLECTED EXPERIENCE,
ALLOWING US TO SKILLFULLY AND COMPASSIONATELY ACT IN THE PRESENT,
RATHER THAN REACT TO THE PAST.

IF YOU'RE NOT GOING TO TELL ME WHAT I WANT TO HEAR, THEN JUST DON'T SAY ANYTHING.
HARUMPF!
WOOF!

OUR PAIN MIRRORS THE PAIN OF ALL BEINGS. WE ARE NOT ALONE.
TOGETHER WE CAN OPEN OUR HEARTS
TO THE HEALING FORCES OF LOVINGKINDNESS.

HIDE AND SEEK OF THE NO SELF.

Mari Gayatri Stein

THE FIBER OF YOUR BEING BECOMES SO SPACIOUS THAT NOTHING IS TRAPPED.

EXPERIENCE THE SPACES.

EMPTINESS IS FULL OF VITALITY. IT HAS SPRINGINESS.

THE SELF LOOKING AT THE SELF.

DIRECT AWARENESS AND CONTINUITY OF EXPERIENCE
GIVE OUR LIFE PURPOSE AND MEANING
AND CREATE A WHOLESOME BALANCE OF EMOTION AND FEELING,
WITH A HEALTHY EXPRESSION OF ENERGY AND EFFORT.

UP? -

DOWN.

WHEN I PAY ATTENTION,
IT GIVES MY LIFE
DIMENSION.

NO!

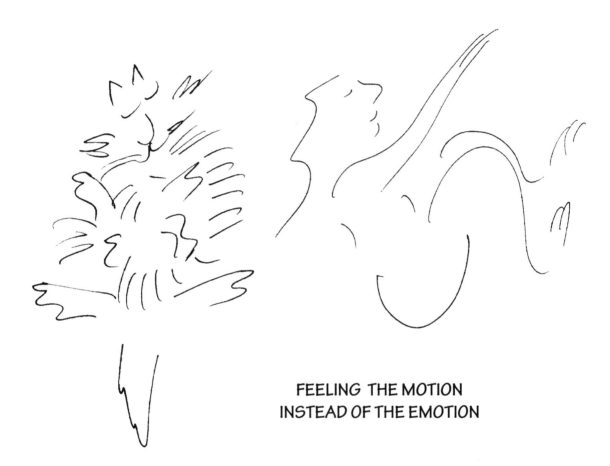

FEELING THE MOTION
INSTEAD OF THE EMOTION

BATHING IN THE WAVES OF ENERGY.

THERE IS NO TIME BUT THE PRESENT.

Chapter Three
The Spiritual Powers and the Precepts

THE FIVE SPIRITUAL POWERS:
FAITH, EFFORT, MINDFULNESS, CONCENTRATION & WISDOM

WE CAN DEVELOP FAITH BY SEEING THAT OTHER PEOPLE HAVE AWAKENED.

FAITH COUNTS

THE BUDDHA SAID TO FIND YOUR OWN TRUTH OF EXPERIENCE.

BELIEVING IN THE BELIEF OF OTHERS WILL HELP SEE US THROUGH TIMES OF SKEPTICISM AND INDECISION. AS WE PRACTICE, WE GATHER EVIDENCE FOR OURSELVES, AND THE TRUTH OF OUR OWN EXPERIENCE DISPELLS OUR DOUBTS.

SEEING ALL EXPERIENCE AS APPEARANCES ARISING
AND VANISHING IN OPEN EMPTINESS OF MIND.

LOOKING THROUGH THE THOUGHT
NOT AT IT.

MAKE A FULL STOP. PAY ATTENTION.

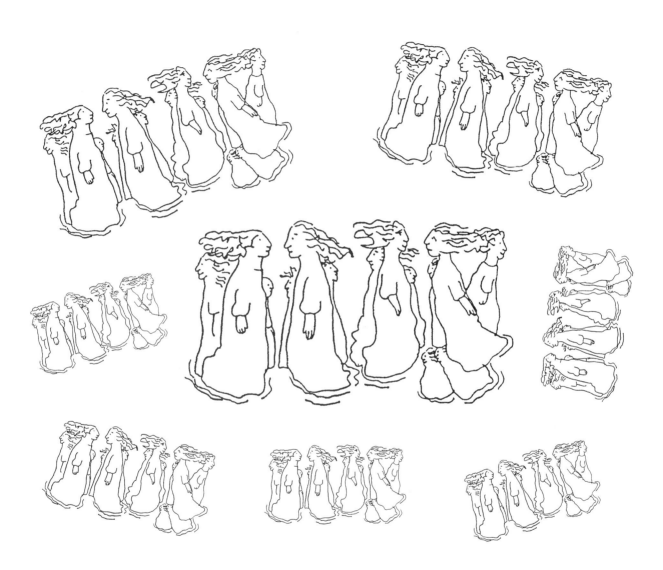

I'LL TAKE A ONE - WAY TICKET BACK HOME TO MYSELF.

Mari Gayatri Stein

LIGHTS, CAMERA, NO ACTION.

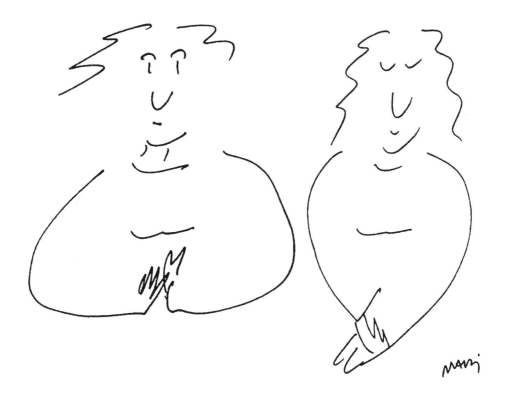

ALERT   TRANQUIL AND ALERT

DO LESS. BE MORE.

TRANQUIL   ALERT AND TRANQUIL

SUFFERING IS WHAT HAPPENS WHEN WE STRUGGLE WITH WHATEVER OUR LIFE EXPERIENCE IS . . .

. . . RATHER THAN OPENING UP TO OUR EXPERIENCE WITH WISE AND COMPASSIONATE RESPONSE

WHY DID I HAVE TO SAY THAT?
I DIDN'T MEAN TO SAY THAT,
IT JUST BURST OUT.

WHEN WE CAUSE HARM,
WE FEEL A WAVE OF TIGHTENING
THROUGHOUT OUR BEING.

shut up shut up shut up shut up shut up shut up shut up shut up
shut up shut up shut up shut up shut up shut up shut up shut up
shut up shut up shut up shut up shut up shut up shut up shut up
shut up shut up shut up shut up shut up shut up shut up shut up
shut up shut up shut up shut up shut up shut up shut up shut up
shut up shut up shut up shut up shut up shut up shut up shut up
shut up shut up shut up shut up shut up shut up shut up shut up
shut up shut up shut up shut up shut up shut up shut up shut up
shut up shut up shut up shut up shut up shut up shut up shut up
shut up shut up shut up shut up shut up shut up shut up shut up
shut up shut up shut up shut up shut up shut up shut up shut up
shut up shut up shut up shut up shut up shut up shut up shut up
shut up shut up shut up shut up shut up shut up shut up shut up
shut up shut up shut up shut up shut up shut up shut up shut up
shut up shut up shut up shut up shut up shut up shut up shut up
shut up shut up shut up shut up shut up shut up shut up shut up
shut up shut up shut up shut up shut up shut up shut up shut
shut up shut up shut up shut up shut up shut up shut up shut
shut up shut up shut up shut up shut up shut up shut up shut
shut up shut up shut up shut up shut up shut up shut up shut
shut up shut up shut up shut up shut up shut up shut up shut
shut up shut up shut up shut up shut up shut up shut up shu
shut up shut up shut up shut up shut up shut up shut up
shut up shut up shut up shut up shut up shut up shut
shut up shut up shut up shut up shut up shut up shut
shut up shut up shut up shut up shut up shut up shut
shut up shut up shut up shut up shut up shut up shut up. HELP

LOOSE LIPS CAUSE SUFFERING,
NOT TO MENTION A LOT OF ENDLESS PAPERWORK.

REFRAINING FROM SPEAKING OF ANY THIRD PERSON NOT PRESENT,
THEIR AFTERNOON SOCIAL ENCOUNTER FELL SOMEWHAT SHORT
OF EXPECTATIONS.

"The law of karma is the light of the world."[1]
Joseph Goldstein

NURTURE THE ROOTS OF HAPPINESS

WHAT CAN HAPPEN WHEN YOU RUN WITH THE MIND AND THE MIND RUNS AMOK.

UNVEILED THREATS

REGARDING GENEROSITY: BEING TERRITORIAL FEELS TERRIBLE.

KARMA STRIKES AGAIN

DOG WALKING ONE WOMAN AND CARRYING ANOTHER

FINDING COMPASSIONATE ALTERNATIVES

NEGOTIATING OVER THE NINE LIVES

"Patience is the sandal which the wise man ties to his feet
rather than cover the whole road with leather."[2]
Lama Mipham

"What's this impatience? As long as you're capable of being annoyed, you can be sure that something will annoy you. When you no longer can be annoyed by little monkeyshines, you'll find most everything agreeable. And of course, you have to watch your own monkeyshines. It's great fun, really. It is! It's fascinating to begin to watch our life unroll and to see what's really going on."[3]
Charlotte Joko Beck

CONSISTENCY IS VITAL. MEDITATE NOW, TALK ON THE PHONE LATER.
MEDITATION IS A LIFE PRACTICE. IF WE WAIT TO MEDITATE UNTIL
CIRCUMSTANCES ARE PERFECT, THE TIME WILL NEVER ARRIVE.

TIME ON THE CUSHION IS CRUCIAL IN DEVELOPING OUR AWARENESS
AND EQUANIMITY, BUT OUR PRACTICE IS LIKE OUR FEET, DESIGNED TO
GO WHERE WE GO AND ABLE TO BRING US BACK HOME TO OUR SELF IF
WE KEEP POINTING THEM IN THE RIGHT DIRECTION.

AIM AND SUSTAIN ATTENTION WITH
THE ONE-POINTED FOCUS OF A BORDER COLLIE.

BYE BYE

REGARDING MINDFULNESS:
JUST KEEP COMING BACK.
JUST BEGIN AGAIN.

A WOMAN WHOSE LIFE TOOK OFF WITHOUT HER.

WE EXPERIENCE A LOT OF GRASPING AROUND THE THINKING PROCESS.

WE HAVE NO PREFERENCE FOR THINKING OR NOT THINKING.
OUR OBJECT IN MEDITATION IS NOT TO STOP THE MIND, BUT TO DEVELOP A
HEALTHY RELATIONSHIP TO THE ART OF THINKING.

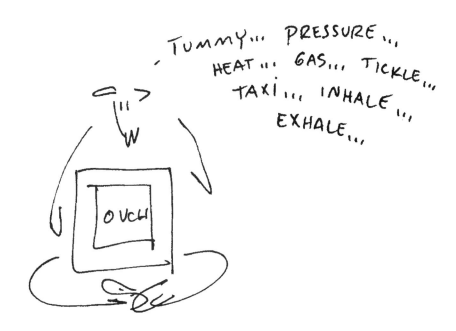

TRY NOTING TO HELP FRAME YOUR FOCUS WHEN THE MIND
ABSCONDS WITH YOU. WHEN YOUR CONCENTRATION IS WELL ESTABLISHED,
YOU CAN DROP THE LABELS AND RETURN TO DIRECT AWARENESS.

SLOW DOWN THE
INTERNAL CLOCK.
BE MATTER-OF-FACT.
OBSERVE WITH DETAIL
AND PRECISION.
NOTICE ANY FEELINGS
OF RELAXATION AND
REPOSE. LABEL OUT
LOUD IN THE FACE
OF RESISTANCE,
DIFFICULT EMOTION
AND PAIN.

SOME THINGS
NEED TO BE
TALKED THROUGH

SOME THINGS NEED
TO BE THOUGHT
THROUGH

SOME CAN ONLY BE
FELT THROUGH

Chapter Four
The Hindrances

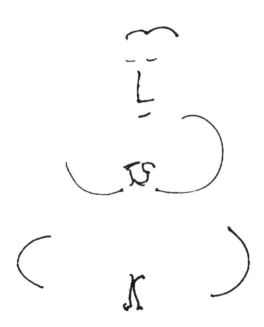

REGARDING THE HINDRANCES
DESIRE
AVERSION
SLEEPINESS
RESTLESSNESS
DOUBT

OBSTACLES TO HAPPINESS
OBSTACLES TO PRACTICE
OBSTACLES TO PARADISE

The Buddha Smiles

FLOATING

CRAVING

DETERMINED

SKEPTICAL

SINKING

AVERSE

AGITATED

CONFUSED

EARNEST

DONT - KNOW - WANNA - KNOW

DOUBTING

THERE ARE SIXTEEN FACES OF MARA IN THIS PICTURE.
CAN YOU SPOT THEM?

THE MIND IS LIKE A PUPPY.

IT WANDERS ENDLESSLY AND DELIGHTS IN EACH NEW DISTRACTION.

WITH AMUSEMENT AND GREAT AFFECTION, PATIENTLY GATHER YOUR MIND BACK AGAIN AND AGAIN AS GENTLY AND LOVINGLY AS YOU WOULD GATHER BACK THIS ADORABLE PUPPY.

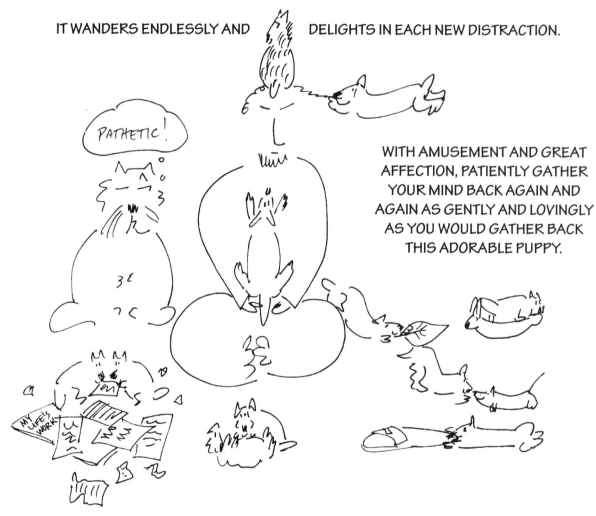

BE GENTLE. DON'T REPRIMAND.

WHEN THERE IS DIALOGUE IN THE MIND, NOTE "TALKING".
WHEN THERE ARE PICTURES IN THE MIND, NOTE "IMAGING".
WHEN THE MIND IS FILLED WITH DOUBT AND
CONFUSION, NOTE "CONFUSION".
WHEN THERE IS MURKY MOVEMENT IN THE MIND, NOTE "SUBTLE".

DISTANCING OURSELVES FROM THE CONTENT OF THOUGHT ALLOWS US TO
REGAIN A SENSE OF OBJECTIVITY AND FREEDOM AND TO PERMIT THE
ESSENCE OF THOUGHT (THE WAVES OF ENERGY) TO MASSAGE THROUGH
THE MIND IN A WHOLESOME WAY.

THOUGHT CAN BE USEFUL.
THOUGHT IS USEFUL WHEN
WE EXPERIENCE IT AS
A MOVING FORCE. IN MEDITATION
WE BEGIN TO WORK THROUGH
THE DRIVING FORCES THAT MAKE
THE MIND THINK.

WHEN YOU FIND YOURSELF DRAWING OUTSIDE THE LINES, USE
NOTING TO HELP BRING YOU BACK TO THE CENTER OF THE PAGE AND
THE MIDDLE WAY. WHEN YOUR CONCENTRATION IS CENTERED IN THE
MIDDLE OF THE PAGE AGAIN, YOU CAN DROP THE LABELS AND
RETURN TO DIRECT AWARENESS.

MOST OF US ARE ADDICTED TO THINKING.
JUST SAY "NO" TO THOUGHT.

WATCH THE WAVES OF THOUGHT INSTEAD OF GETTING
CAUGHT UP IN THE CONTENT OF THOUGHT.

WHEN THERE
ARE VOICES,
WHOSE VOICES?

WHEN THERE ARE
IMAGES,
WHOSE IMAGES?

WHO IS LISTENING?
WHO IS TALKING?

LISTEN TO THE CADENCE OF THOUGHT AS THOUGH LISTENING
TO A DISTANT SOUND IN A FOREIGN TONGUE .

THE ARE YOU LISTENING MINDFULNESS TEST.

BEING PRECISE IN YOUR
AWARENESS HELPS TO TEASE
APART THE TANGLING OF THOUGHTS
AND FEELINGS AND TO DISPELL
THE ILLUSION OF THEIR SOLIDNESS.

FEELINGS ARE AS EPHEMERAL AS THE WEATHER.
MEDITATION ALLOWS US TO RIDE OUT THE STORMS GRACEFULLY
WHILE WE BASK IN THE LIGHT OF OUR AWARENESS.

WALKING MEDITATION IS DESIGNED TO SO COMPLETELY FLOOD YOUR
CONSCIOUSNESS WITH REALITY MOMENTS THAT THERE SIMPLY IS NO
TIME LEFT FOR GRASPING AND FREEZING.

THIS TOO SHALL PASS.

AU CONTRAIRE
THIS IS
PASSING NOW
IN THIS
VERY MOMENT
OF OUR AWARENESS.

REGARDING ANGER
LET IT OUT, BUT DON'T SET IT LOOSE.

"When you give in to aversion and anger, it's as though, having decided to kill someone by throwing him into a river, you wrap your arms around his neck, jump into the water with him, and you both drown. In destroying your enemy, you destroy yourself as well."[1]
Chagbud Tulku Rinpoche

WHEN DOGMA MEETS DHARMA.

WHEW!

I'LL JUST SNEAK A PEEK? WHOODS.. AHEM.

TAIL .. INFLATING .. COTTON CANDY .. JELLO JIGGLING .. MOLTEN LAVA FLOWING .. TAXI .. BIG BALLOON ABOUT TO GO BANG ..

WHEN A SENSE OF PHYSICAL DISTORTION ARISES, I INFUSE IT WITH AWARENESS AND EXPLORE THE SPECIFIC SENSATIONS AND IMAGES WITH MINDFULNESS AND EQUANIMITY. SOMETIMES I OPEN MY EYES BRIEFLY TO REORIENT MYSELF.

REGARDING EATING MEDITATION

"Eat slowly and mindfully, even if you become impatient and driven to gobble. If this should happen, be grateful, it represents a significant opportunity to work through driveness and achieve more ease in daily life."[2]
Shinzen Young

The Buddha Smiles

At the dining room table
we observe ourselves / we hear what we are saying
we hear what they are saying
how we sound / how we think we sound
what they really mean / how we look / if we have pepper in our teeth
(we discreetly run our tongue over our teeth)
we remind ourselves not to smile / we don't feel like smiling anyhow
we are overwhelmed, hopeless, defeated, embarrassed, self-pitying
we think about stabbing ourselves with the bread knife
(we consider the effect)
we think about stabbing them with the bread knife
we fantasize the whole affair
the drama!!!
the blood-stained napkin clutched in white knuckles!!!
our host's head fallng forward into the hollandaise sauce
we smile
we feel guilty about not feeling guilty
we feel like the overcooked brussels sprouts in the center of the table
we feel ridiculous and angry because we don't take ourselves seriously
we feel vulnerable / we wonder if they feel vulnerable too
suddenly we feel starved
we request a second helping of chocolate cake and rum raisin ice cream
we gobble it down and after we do
we observe ourselves / we observe them
we observe them observing us observing ourselves

AT THE DINING ROOM TABLE

WE OBSERVE OURSELVES / WE OBSERVE THEM
WE OBSERVE THEM OBSERVING US OBSERVING OURSELVES

ANY TENSION OR COMPULSIVENESS SHOULD BE CONSCIOUSLY LET
GO OF RATHER THAN IGNORED BY DIVERTING ATTENTION.

WHEN YOU OVEREAT, IT FEELS LIKE
SOMETHING CONCRETE TO HATE YOURSELF FOR...

I COMPLETELY
DON'T KNOW,
THEREFORE, I AM
INTUITIVELY
WISE.

CLARITY, WISDOM AND INSIGHT
RESULT WHEN WE HAVE
A COMPLETE EXPERIENCE OF THE
DON'T-KNOW-MIND.

THE SUBTLE IS SIGNIFICANT AND POWERFUL.

EXPERIENCE DOESN'T HAVE TO BE EXTREME TO BE EFFECTIVE AND LIBERATING, BUT IT DOES HAVE TO BE COMPLETE.

QUALITY NOT QUANTITY.

MEDITATION ALLOWS US TO CHANGE OUR
POINT OF VIEW AND BASIC RELATIONSHIP
TO EXPERIENCE.

FROM HOLES TO WHOLENESS.

I KNOW THAT FEAR
IS A MIND STUMBLE.
I CAN TELL MYSELF,
I'M FRIGHTENED NOW
BECAUSE EVEN THOUGH
I KNOW WHAT IS TRUE,
AND I'VE FORGOTTEN
IT RIGHT NOW, I KNOW
THAT THE POSSIBILITY
OF REMEMBERING
EXISTS.

IN MEDITATION, WE GET TO
REINVENT OURSELVES WITH THE
ARISING OF EACH NEW MOMENT.

GEE, I FEEL GOOD TODAY.
I WONDER WHAT'S WRONG WITH ME.
MAYBE I'M IN DENIAL. MAYBE I
SHOULDN'T FEEL SO GOOD - IT MIGHT
JINX THINGS. PEOPLE ARE SUFFERING
IN THE WORLD AND I HAVE THE
AUDACITY TO SIT HERE AND FEEL GOOD.

BUT I AM WORRIED ABOUT FEELING
TOO GOOD. IT MAKES ME AFRAID
THAT SOMETHING
REALLY BAD
IS GOING TO
HAPPEN AND
THEN I'LL
FEEL EVEN
WORSE.

GEEZ, I'M UNGRATEFUL. NOW I FEEL SO GUILTY.
I THINK I'LL JUST SIT HERE AND ENJOY FEELING GOOD....

... BUT I CAN'T.
IT'S ALL RUINED,
BECAUSE NOW I
FEEL BAD ABOUT
FEELING
TOO GOOD

INSTEAD OF JUST ENJOYING FEELING GOOD WHEN I KNOW
LIFE IS IMPERMANENT AND IT WILL CHANGE ANYWAY.
SO REALLY IT DOESN'T MAKE MUCH SENSE TO FEEL BAD.
SO I MIGHT AS WELL FEEL GOOD WHILE FEELING GOOD
IS AN OPTION, BECAUSE WHO KNOWS WHAT FATE WILL
BEFALL US ALL TOMORROW?

OKAY THEN. HERE I AM, FEELING GOOD.
BUT I FEEL LIKE A REAL PUDDIN' WASTING
ALL THIS TIME ON THINKING ABOUT FEELINGS
INSTEAD OF REALLY FEELING THEM.
AND TIME IS RUNNING OUT ON ALL OF US.
I'M AFRAID I'M WASTING TOO MUCH TIME
ON UNIMPORTANT THINGS. I SHOULD BE
OUT THERE DOING SOMETHING USEFUL.

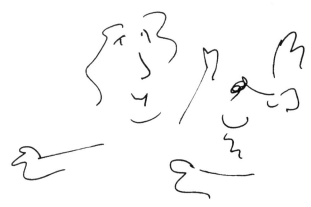

BUT I'M AFRAID, AND I KNOW THAT
I SHOULD REALLY BE ABLE TO
OVERCOME FEAR AND REPLACE IT
WITH FAITH OR FEEL IT DISSOLVE
INTO ITS PURE ESSENCE OF ENERGY.
YES, THAT'S JUST WHAT I'LL DO.
HERE, I'LL CLOSE MY EYES AND
BECOME A FEARLESS PERSON.

WELL, DO I LOOK FEARLESS NOW?
I HAVE AN OVERWHELMING URGE TO LICK YOU ON THE NOSE.

SIGH. I'M REALLY JUST HOPELESS. NOW I FEEL ANGRY AT MYSELF FOR BEING SO USELESS, AND NOT HAVING ENOUGH FAITH TO OVERCOME MY FEAR. I'M REALLY MAD AT ME..

HOW CAN YOU HAVE SELF-ESTEEM WHEN THERE IS NO SELF?

THAT MAKES ME AN ANGRY PERSON, AND I DON'T LIKE ANGRY PEOPLE ANGRY PEOPLE AREN'T NICE. SIGH. I WONDER IF I'LL EVER BE NORMAL. SELF-ESTEEM, THAT'S WHAT I NEED — SELF-ESTEEM.

OH, THAT'S RIGHT. I FORGOT. GEE!!! YOU KNOW, I FEEL GOOD. I REALLY FEEL GOOD.

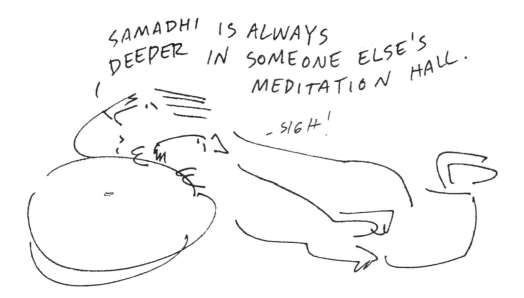

THE EIGHT WORLDLY DRAMAS,
I MEAN DHARMAS.

"Becoming immersed in the four pairs of opposites: pleasure and pain, loss and gain, fame and disgrace, and praise and blame is what keeps us stuck in the pain of samsara. We can already see that many of our mood swings are related to how we interpret what happens. If we look closely at our mood swings, we'll notice that something always sets them off. The irony is that we make up the eight worldly dharmas. We make them up in reaction to what happens to us in this world. They are nothing concrete in themselves. The eight worldly dharmas can become a means for growing wiser as well as kinder and more content."[3]
Pema Chodron

i.e. VICISSITUDES~CHEESE TODAY, GONE TOMORROW,

PLEASURE AND PAIN

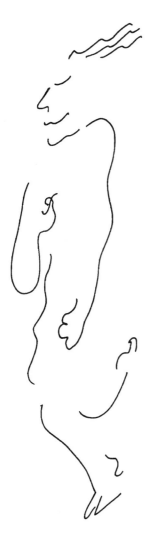

LOSS AND GAIN

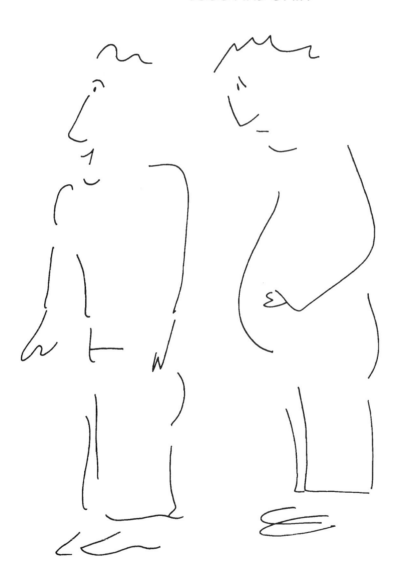

PRAISE AND BLAME

Mari Gayatri Stein

FAME

AND ILL REPUTE

Mari Gayatri Stein

NO PLACE
TO GET TO.
NOTHING TO DO.

Chapter Five
Vipassana:
The Practice of Insight into Our True Nature

IN A SINGLE MOMENT OF UNDERSTANDING
ALL BECOMES CLEAR

REGARDING MINDFULNESS

Beginner's Mind

WHEN SPIRITUALITY IS IN THE THINKING MIND,
IT LEADS TO OPINIONS AND CONFLICT.
WHEN SPIRITUALITY IS CENTERED IN THE HEART,
FEELINGS OF PIETY AND DEVOTION ARISE
AND LEAD TO TRUE UNDERSTANDING.

Big Mind

WE ARE INTERDEPENDENT BEINGS.
EVERY BREATH IS AN EXCHANGE OF ENERGY.

THE RECIPROCITY OF BREATH WITH MOTHER NATURE.
NO PREFERENCE FOR INHALING OR EXHALING.

YOU ARE HELD IN THE EMBRACE OF MOTHER NATURE.
ANCHORED BY THE EARTH AND CARESSED BY THE ETHERS.
YOUR POSTURE IS AS THOUGH YOU ARE GENTLY BALANCING
A THOUSAND-PETALED LOTUS ON THE TOP OF YOUR HEAD
WHILE YOUR TAILBONE SUBTLY REACHES FOR THE EARTH,
AS THOUGH SENDING ROOTS INTO THE GROUND.

HAPPINESS IS FRAGILE.
TAKE GREAT CARE OF ALL THAT YOU DO.

WE ARE THE ESSENCE.

LIFE IS A DANCE
AND MOTHER NATURE IS YOUR PARTNER.
FOLLOW HER RHYTHMS
AND WHATEVER YOU DO,
DON'T STEP ON HER TOES.

MEDITATION CREATES AN ENVIRONMENT WHERE THE KNOTS
OF OLD CONDITIONED RESPONSE UNTIE THEMSELVES,
AND THE BLOCKAGES TO HAPPINESS
— MENTALLLY, PHYSICALLY AND SPIRITUALLY —
SPONTANEOUSLY DISSOLVE.
THE TIGHTENINGS, TENSIONS AND MEMORIES PERCOLATE UP AND OUT
OF THE BODY NATURALLY AND THE EFFULGENT SELF SHINES THROUGH.

WHEN I WAS A LITTLE GIRL, I USED TO THINK
THERE WERE LIONS UNDER MY BED.
EVERY NIGHT MY MOTHER WOULD COME IN AND
SCARE THEM AWAY. NOW THE LIONS ARE
IN MY HEAD AND THEY ARE GROWING OLD WITH ME.

POLISHING THE POT

STILL VERY MURKY!

BE DOGGED ABOUT YOUR PRACTICE AND FULL OF ZEAL.

ACTIVE

REACTIVE

BE RECEPTIVE RATHER THAN CONCEPTIVE,
ACTIVE RATHER THAN REACTIVE.
MEDITATION IS A SPIRITUAL WORKOUT.
YOU ARE PULLED AWAY A TRILLION TIMES
AND COME BACK A TRILLION AND ONE.
DEVELOP YOUR SPIRITUAL MUSCLES.

WE ARE MARRIED TO OUR WORK.

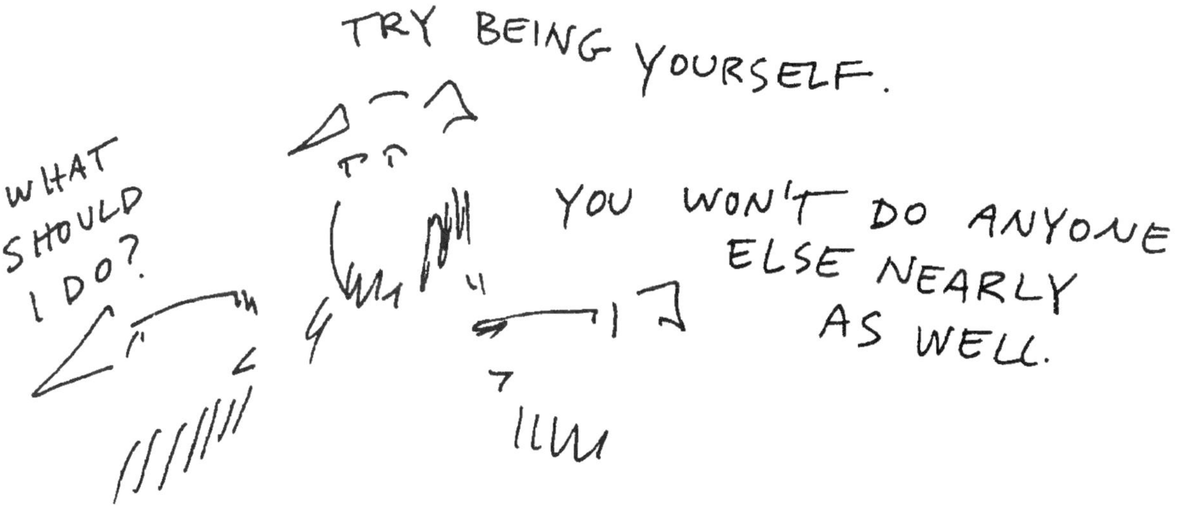

TRY BEING YOURSELF.

WHAT SHOULD I DO?

YOU WON'T DO ANYONE ELSE NEARLY AS WELL.

REVELING IN THE FREEDOM OF NON-DUALITY.

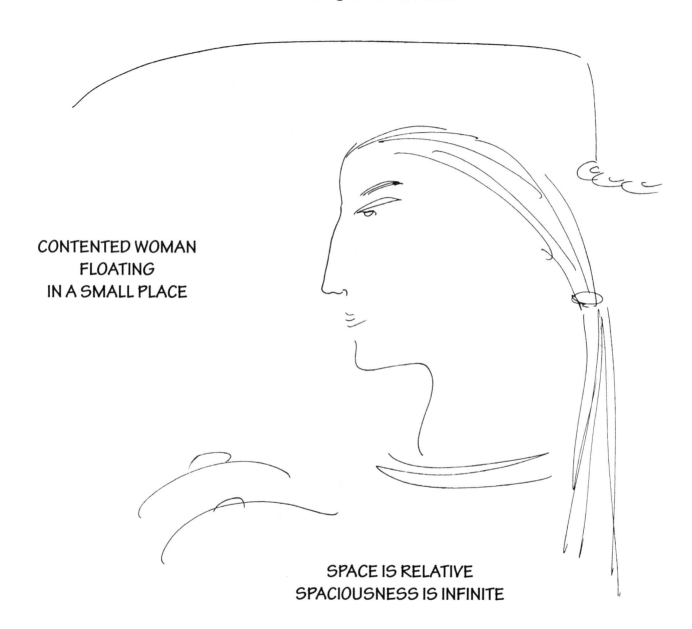

CONTENTED WOMAN
FLOATING
IN A SMALL PLACE

SPACE IS RELATIVE
SPACIOUSNESS IS INFINITE

NOTICING THE MIND FLAVOR OF FEELINGS

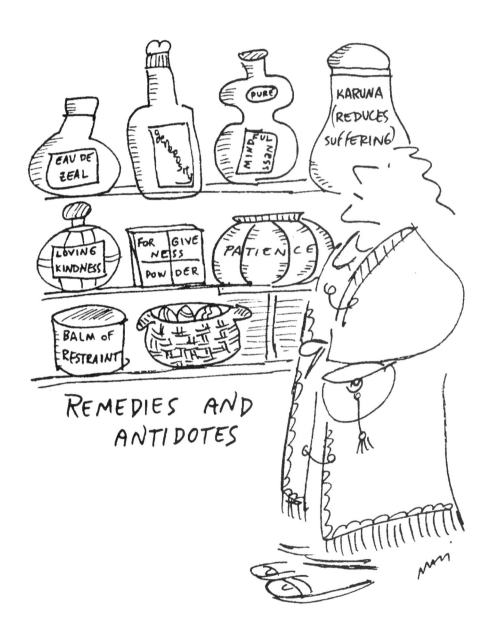

LIVING INSIDE THAT FLOWER.
DWELLING IN THE COMPLETE
EXPERIENCE OF THE FLOWER.
WHEN WE COME BACK HOME
TO OURSELVES,
NOTHING IS MISSING.
EVERYTHING IS STILL THERE.
WE LEARN TO FIND PEACE IN THE
REFUGE WITHIN.

Mari Gayatri Stein

THE COMPLETE EXPERIENCE OF DOG.

STRIVING FAILS AGAIN

PHYSICAL HAPPINESS

WHEN ENERGY MOVES,
IT STIRS THE NECTAR AND FEELS DELICIOUS.

DISCERNING THAT "JUST RIGHT" PLACE IN ALL THAT WE DO.
NOT TOO MUCH. NOT TOO LITTLE. JUST RIGHT.

NOT TOO FAST. NOT TOO SLOW. JUST RIGHT.
HAPPINESS IS KNOWING THAT "JUST RIGHT" PLACE.

SO STILL YOU CAN SEE A FLOWER OPEN.

SO ATTENTIVE YOU CAN FEEL YOUR FORM CHANGE.

THE MUSIC
PLAYS ITSELF
THROUGH YOU.

DOG AND HER FAITHFUL COMPANION RETURNING TO NATURE.

REGARDING SIMPLE HAPPINESS

THE BLISS OF DIRECT EXPERIENCE

Mari Gayatri Stein

BEING STILL AND STILL BEING.

JUST SITTING AND WATCHING, NOT TRYING TO DO ANYTHING,
NOT EVEN WAITING.

INSIGHTS OF A MEDITATING SWIMMER.

STAND STILL
TAKE A BREATH
RELAX
PAY ATTENTION, LOVING ATTENTION

DRINK OF LIFE BUT DON'T GUZZLE.
SPEND YOUR ENERGY MORE CAREFULLY THAN YOU SPEND YOUR MONEY.
HOW MUCH DOES A MOMENT OF MINDLESSNESS REALLY COST?
IF YOU WERE STRANDED IN THE DESERT WITH ONLY A LITTLE WATER,
HOW PRECIOUS WOULD EACH SIP BE?
RECYCLE YOUR ENERGY, NOT JUST YOUR NEWSPAPERS.

MAY YOUR HEART
BE FULL AND
YOUR SELF
BE EMPTY.

IF THERE IS NOTHING
OUTSIDE THE SELF, THEN
THERE IS NOTHING TO
FEAR, NOTHING TO
DESIRE, TO BE MAD AT,
TO COMPETE WITH, TO
STRIVE FOR. AS I OPEN
COMPLETELY TO EACH
MOMENT ARISING AND
PASSING AWAY, I SEE THAT I AM
VIRTUALLY EMPTY
OF SELF IN A
SPACE WHERE
THERE IS
NOTHING BUT
SELF.

Falling Into Your Own Arms At Last

Dreams and delusions are dashed
The illusory bubble of protection
      has burst
There is nothing but spaciousness
Space is good
Space is wonderful
It's just a bit tricky learning how to relax
after all these years

Stop clawing the air
Ease your grip
Decontract and become lofty
Let yourself be liberated by the space
Heir to the ethers

How do you fall effortlessly
And ecstatically
Moment to moment
In this vast translucence
With no north or south
East or west
Up or down
In or out

Now the emptiness full of heart *called life*
Dissolves through the darkness and light
Of the mysterious emptiness *called death*
Fear, the congealing foe, cannot be held at bay
But can be worn like a life jacket
The transmuting of each difficulty
Becomes the energy, the wave that
      carries you along
To those shores of right seeing

With each blink of an eye
And with each breath

Alas and hurrah
There is nothing left to figure out
Just a leap into this
Circle of infinite compassion
Its color so pale it is invisible
But the eye will still see
The ocean and the sky as deep blue
Embrace the blueness
Even as you gaze through its
      transparency
Court the moment
Don your best gear
Let Mother Nature caress you
There is no other lover to satisfy you now
Resist nothing.
You cannot, can you?

CHAPTER SIX
METTA:
THE ART OF LOVINGKINDNESS

THE METTA RESSOLVES

MAY I BE FREE OF DANGER

MAY I
HAVE MENTAL
HAPPINESS

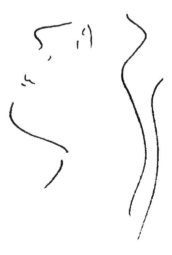

MAY I HAVE
PHYSICAL HAPPINESS

MAY WE HAVE EASE OF WELL BEING

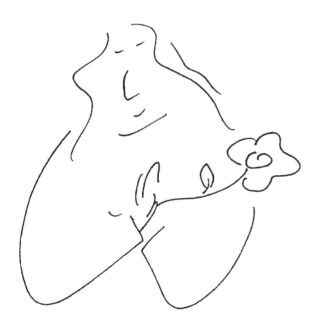

WE BEGIN BY SENDING WISHES
OF HAPPINESS AND WELL-BEING
TO OURSELVES

SO PLEASED WITH YOURSELF

AN OCEAN OF DEVOTION

WE EXTEND THE WISHES OF WELL-BEING
TO A BENEFACTOR AND THOSE WE LOVE

WE ARE ABLE TO GO ON
AND WISH WELL TO THOSE WITH WHOM
WE HAVE HAD CONFLICTS

HMMM — MORE HEAVENLY STUFF — ABODES, THIS TIME.

1- LOVINGKINDNESS
2- COMPASSION
3- SYMPATHETIC JOY
4- EQUANIMITY

MAY WE BE UNSHAKABLE IN OUR COMMITMENT TO OUR OWN TRUTH (BUT FLUID AS WE MOVE THROUGH THE WORLD.

AT OUR OWN (PACE.

BRAHMA VIHARAS

MUDITA TRIUMPHS IN THE FACE OF ENVY

NON-INTERFERENCE IS THE BEST POLICY

EXPECT THE BEST
JUST DON'T BE TOO SPECIFIC
EXPECTATIONS CAN BE REAL TRAPS

Mari Gayatri Stein

WE BEGIN TO HAVE COMPASSION FOR
ALL THE SUFFERING
IN ALL THE HEARTS
OF ALL THE BEINGS
IN ALL THE REALMS
AND ALL THE FORMS

MAY YOU AND ALL THE SERPENTS EVERYWHERE (LONG OR SHORT, BIG OR SMALL, POISONOUS OR NON-POISONOUS, SCALY OR SMOOTH, COLORFUL OR BLAND, HERE OR THERE, HATCHED OR UNHATCHED) BE FREE OF PAIN AND SUFFERING. MAY WE ALL BE AT PEACE.

IF I HAVE HURT OR HARMED ANYONE KNOWINGLY OR UNKNOWINGLY, I ASK THEIR FORGIVENESS. IF ANYONE HAS HURT OR HARMED ME KNOWINGLY OR UNKNOWINGLY, I FORGIVE THEM.

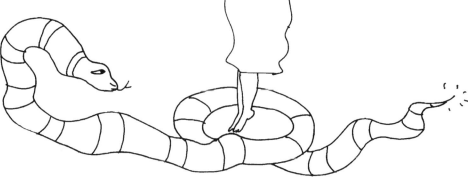

FORGIVENESS
IS AT THE HEART
OF ALL HAPPINESS

MAY ALL BEINGS BE HAPPY AND SECURE; MAY THEIR MINDS BE CONTENTED.

Metta is a protection
against the heart shattering
as a result of those natural vicissitudes of life.
It softens the heart.
The heart feels but it does not shatter.
Metta softens the heart. [1]
Sylvia Boorstein

WE BEGIN TO OPEN UP AND TURN TOWARD
DIFFICULT EMOTIONS AND FEELINGS
RATHER THAN TIGHTENING UP AND TURNING AWAY,
ALLOWING THEM TO BREAK UP INTO AN ENERGY FLOW,
THEN WE CAN COLOR THEM WITH
LOVINGKINDNESS, PLEASURE AND COMPASSION.

VIEWING THE ABSENCE OF INTERNAL VOICE AS PERIODS OF PEACE

SILA MEANS MORAL, NOT MORALISTIC.
DON'T BE A GOODY-TWO-PAWS.
JUST BE A GOOD DOG.

TOO GOOD TO BE TRUE

OUR SPIRITUAL SOURCE PULLS ON US WITH A GRAVITATIONAL FORCE.
OUR PRACTICE SPEEDS US ALONG THE WAY.
WE ARE PART OF THE WHOLE SPECTRUM OF MYSTICS,
MAKING THE JOURNEY FROM THE NATURE OF CONSCIOUSNESS
TO THE SOURCE OF CONSCIOUSNESS.
A BRIDGE FROM THE FINITE TO THE INFINITE.

LET THE ICE OF YOUR EGO MELT.

DROP THE IMAGE AND STOP APOLOGIZING
FOR BEING A FRIENDLY PERSON.

BETTER TO BE THE ONE WHO SMILED,
THAN THE ONE WHO DIDN'T SMILE BACK.

THE SUPPORT OF KINDRED SPIRITS IS A BOON TO PRACTICE.

IMPROVISING WITH METTA

MAY MY BOWL BE FULL AND MY SELF BE EMPTY.

MORGAN

MAY WE BE HEALTHY AND WHOLE,
FREE OF PAIN AND SUFFERING,
ACCEPTING, HEALED, VITAL
AND RESTED, FREE
OF FATIGUE AND
FULL OF ENERGY,
FREE OF
RESISTANCE
AND FULL OF
ACCEPTANCE
FREE OF
FEAR AND
FULL OF
FAITH
FREE OF
DOUBT AND
FULL OF GRATITUDE.

— VERBOSE —
BUT STILL
SO CUTE.

FROM THE HEAD TO THE HEART

THE MILLINER OF MIND STATES

METTA MACHINE (BATTERIES INCLUDED)
FOR THE ONE WHO HAS EVERYTHING
BUT STILL ISN'T SATISFIED.

VIOLATORS WILL BE RELENTLESSLY
BOMBARDED WITH LOVING RESOLVES

GIVING UNTIL IT FEELS HARMLESS

AN ACT OF GENEROSITY IS LIKE A SMILE THROUGH THE WHOLE BODY.

Mari Gayatri Stein

WHOOPS ! METTAROTE.

WHEN MOMMY GETS HOME FROM HER METTA RETREAT

Mari Gayatri Stein

Menu de Metta
Compote of
Contentment
Assorted
Mixture of
Happy Greens
(Organic)
Tureen of
Well being
Peace
Pie

ENJOYING A METTA MEAL
SAVORING EACH AND EVERY MORSEL

STRETCHING WITH THE PLEASURE
OF AN ANIMAL STRETCHING IN THE SUN

THE COMPLETE EXPERIENCE OF PLEASURE
WITH MINDFULNESS AND EQUANIMITY
CAN PERMANENTLY ELEVATE OUR CAPACITY FOR JOY

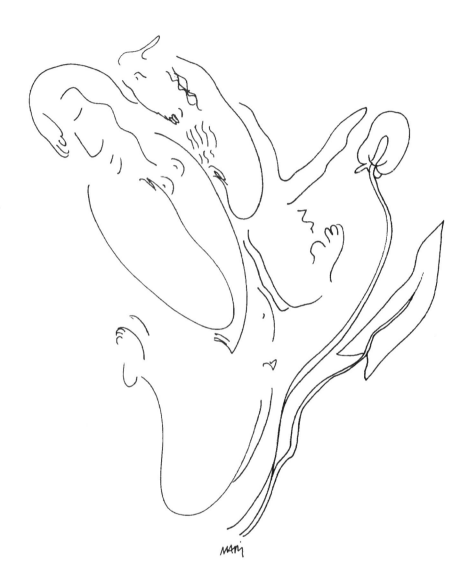

THE COMFORT OF A LOVED ONE

NOTHING TO DO, NOTHING TO CHANGE.

- EVERYTHING PERFECT, JUST AS IT IS.

HAPPINESS CANNOT BE FOUND
THROUGH GREAT EFFORT AND WILLPOWER,
BUT IS ALREADY PRESENT, IN OPEN RELAXATION AND LETTING GO.

DON'T STRAIN YOURSELF,
THERE IS NOTHING TO DO OR UNDO.
WHATEVER MOMENTARILY ARISES IN THE BODY-MIND
HAS NO REAL IMPORTANCE AT ALL,
HAS LITTLE REALITY WHATSOEVER.
WHY IDENTIFY WITH, AND BECOME ATTACHED TO IT,
PASSING JUDGMENT UPON IT AND OURSELVES?

FAR BETTER TO SIMPLY
LET THE ENTIRE GAME HAPPEN ON ITS OWN,
SPRINGING UP AND FALLING BACK LIKE WAVES-
WITHOUT CHANGING OR MANIPULATING ANYTHING-
AND NOTICE HOW EVERYTHING VANISHES AND
REAPPEARS, MAGICALLY, AGAIN AND AGAIN,
TIME WITHOUT END.

The Buddha Smiles

ONLY OUR SEARCHING FOR HAPPINESS
PREVENTS US FROM SEEING IT.
IT IS LIKE A VIVID RAINBOW WHICH YOU PURSUE WITHOUT EVER CATCHING.

OR A DOG CHASING ITS OWN TAIL.

ALTHOUGH PEACE AND HAPPINESS DO NOT EXIST
AS AN ACTUAL THING OR PLACE,
THEY ARE ALWAYS AVAILABLE
AND ACCOMPANY YOU EVERY INSTANT.

DON'T BELIEVE IN THE REALITY
OF GOOD AND BAD EXPERIENCES;
THEY ARE LIKE TODAY'S EPHEMERAL WEATHER,
LIKE RAINBOWS IN THE SKY.

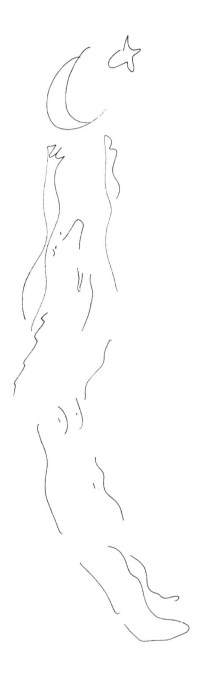

WANTING TO GRASP THE UNGRASPABLE
YOU EXHAUST YOURSELF IN VAIN.

AS SOON AS YOU OPEN AND RELAX
THIS TIGHT FIST OF GRASPING,
INFINITE SPACE IS THERE -OPEN,
INVITING AND COMFORATBLE.

The Buddha Smiles

MAKE USE OF THIS SPACIOUSNESS, THIS FREEDOM AND NATURAL EASE.
DON'T SEARCH ANY FURTHER,
DON'T GO INTO THE TANGLED JUNGLE
LOOKING FOR THE GREAT AWAKENED ELEPHANT,

WHO IS ALREADY RESTING QUIETLY AT HOME
IN FRONT OF YOUR OWN HEARTH.

NOTHING TO DO OR UNDO,
NOTHING TO FORCE,
NOTHING TO WANT,
AND NOTHING MISSING —

EMAHO! MARVELOUS!
EVERYTHING HAPPENS BY ITSELF.

EMAHO

"Now come up close and listen. When you look carefully, you won't find the merest speck of Real Mind you can put your finger on and say, "This is it!" And not finding anything is an incredible find. Friends! To start with, Mind does not emerge from anything. It's primordially empty; there's nothing there to hold on to. It isn't anywhere; it has no shape or colour. And in the end nowhere to go. There's no trace of its having been. Its movements are empty, but that emptiness is apparent. In the beginning Mind itself is not created by causes. And finally not destroyed by external conditions. It neither grows nor gets stuck. It's not empty or full. Infusing peace and anguish alike, it shows no preference. Ceaselessly it reveals itself as everything so you can't say "Here it is!" Not being fixed as something, it's beyond presence and absence. It neither comes nor goes, gets born nor dies, illuminates nor . . . obscures. Mind's nature is vivid as a flawless piece of crystal: intrinsically empty, naturally radiant, ceaselessly responsive. Stripped bare of samsaric error, Mind itself is surely and always Buddha."
Shabkar (1781-1851)

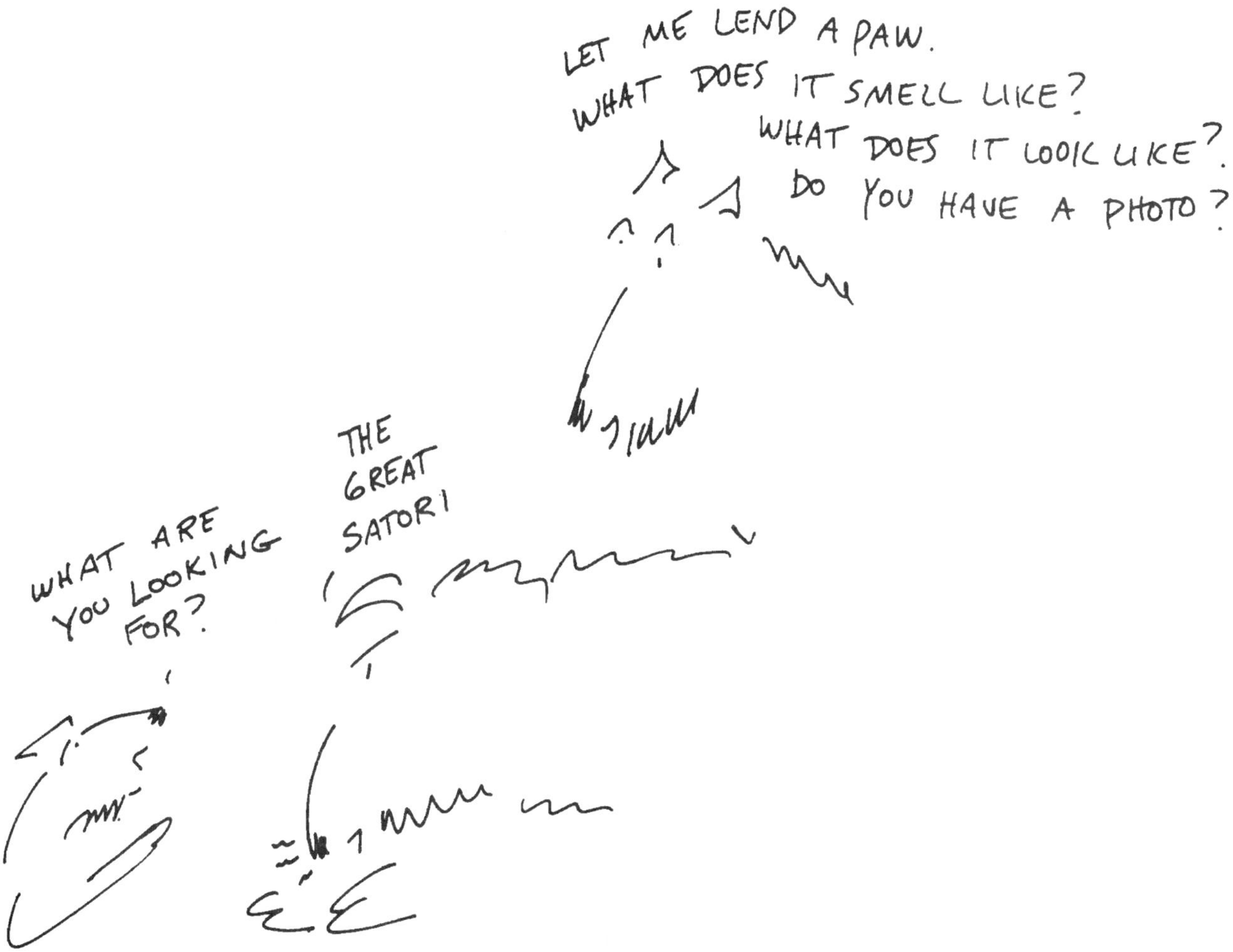

LET ME LEND A PAW.
WHAT DOES IT SMELL LIKE?
WHAT DOES IT LOOK LIKE?
DO YOU HAVE A PHOTO?

THE
GREAT
SATORI

WHAT ARE
YOU LOOKING
FOR?

Great satori doesn't just fall out of the skies.[2]
Charlotte Joko Beck

COMPLETELY BREATHING, COMPLETELY LIVING.

I BREATHE AS THOUGH THIS IS MY FIRST BREATH.
AND I BREATHE AS THOUGH THIS IS MY LAST BREATH.

MAY YOUR HEARTS BE FULL
AND YOUR BALLOONS BE EMPTY

This is what should be done
By those who are skilled in goodness,
And who know the path of peace:
Let them be able and upright,
Straightforward and gentle in speech.
Humble and not conceited,
Contented and easily satisfied.
Unburdened with duties and frugal in their ways.
Peaceful and calm, and wise and skillful,
Not proud and demanding in nature.
Let them not do the slightest thing
That the wise would later reprove.
Wishing: in gladness and in safety,
May all beings be at ease.
Whatever living beings there may be;
Whether they are weak or strong, omitting none,
The great or the mighty, medium, short or small,
The seen and the unseen,
Those living near and far away,
Those born and to-be-born
May all beings be at ease!
Let none deceive another,
Or despise any being in any state.

Let none through anger or ill-will
Wish harm upon another.
Even as a mother protects with her life
Her child, her only child,
So with a boundless heart
Should One cherish all living beings;
Radiating kindness over the entire world:
Spreading upward to the skies,
And downward to the depths;
Outward and unbounded,
Freed from hatred and ill-will.
Whether standing or walking, seated or lying down,
Free from drowsiness,
One should sustain this recollection.
This is said to be the sublime abiding.
By not holding to fixed views,
The pure-hearted one, having clarity of vision,
Being freed from all sense desires,
Is not born again into the world.[3]

The Metta Sutta, the Buddha's words on lovingkindness

Mari Gayatri Stein

MAY ALL BEINGS
IN ALL REALMS
IN ALL FORMS
BE FREE OF PAIN AND SUFFERING
MAY WE ALL BE AT PEACE

NOTES

Chapter 1

1. PemaChodron, *When Things Fall Apart* (Boston, Shambhala Publications, 1997), pp. 53-54.

2.Charlotte Joko Beck, "Life's Not A Problem," *Tricycle* (Summer 1998), p. 37.

3. Gil Fronsdal, *Voices from Spirit Rock*, (Rancho Cordova: CA: Spirit Rock Center, 1996), p. 89.

4. Sylvia Boorstein, personal communication with the author.

Chapter 2

1. Sylvia Boorstein, personal communication with the author.

2. Pema Chodron, *When Things Fall Apart*, pp. 53, 55, 59.

Chapter 3

1. Joseph Goldstein in Susan Salzberg and Joseph Goldstein, *Insight Meditation* (Louisville: CO: Sounds True, 1998).

2. Lama Mipham, *Calm and Clear* (Emeryville, Calif.: Dharma Publishing, 1973), p. 31.

3. Charlotte Joko Beck, "Life's Not a Problem," *Tricycle* (Summer 1998), p. 37.

Chapter 4

1. Chagbud Tulku Rinpoche, "Putting Down the Arrow," *Tricycle* (Summer 1998), p. 56.

2. Shinzen Young, personal communication with the author.

3. Pema Chodron, *When Things Fall Apart*, p. 54.

Chapter 6

1. Sylvia Boorstein, personal communication with the author.

2. Charlotte Joko Beck, "Life's Not a Problem," p. 37.

3. Quoted in Sharon Salzberg, *Loving Kindness: The Revolutionary Art of Happiness* (Boston: Shambhala Publications, 1995), pp. vii-viii.

GLOSSARY

Bodhisattva: (Bodhi = the perfection of insight and wisdom; Sattva = truth)

An enlightenment being. An awakened heart and one who is on the path of enlightenment .

Brahma Viharas: Divine Abodes

The divine states of mind in which a *bodhisattva* dwells radiating these four blissful qualities like the warming rays of the sun.

Metta (*maitra* — infinite lovingkindness towards all)

Karuna (infinite compassion towards all)

Mudita (sympathetic joy in the happiness and liberation of all)

Upeksha (infinite equanimity towards all and a perfect impartial view of all experience)

Buddha:

The awakened or enlightened one, the founder of Buddhism. The historical Buddha, Prince Siddhartha Gautama (attained goal, best on earth) was born in the foothills of the Himalayas in the sixth century B.C.E. Astrologers had predicted that Siddhartha would become either a great king or a great holy man. His father wished for his son to rule after him and tried to shelter Siddhartha from the harshness of the world beyond the palace gates. The king lavished his heir with every imaginable enjoyment and amusement that he may remain contented and committed to the worldly life. But it was to no avail. Although forbidden by his father, Siddhartha convinced his charioteer to take him out into the world, leaving the protection of his royal home for

the first time. The prince encountered someone old, someone sick, someone dead, and someone holy. On witnessing the great suffering of humanity and transitory nature of life, this sage of the Shakya Clan abandoned the life of a royal and became an ascetic. He under-took many severe austerities and finally settled down under the famous bodhi tree, determined to be liberated and to discover the way to the end of suffering. *Shakyamuni buddha* (the awakened one) faced all the demons and torments of mind and matter and attained enlightenment. From the time of his great awakening, he traveled all over India teaching the experience of liberation, the middle path, embodied in the four noble truths in the language of Pali. His disciples later committed the Buddha's conversational teachings to paper.

Dana:

Donation, benevolent giving of alms, charity and self-yielding for the happiness of all sentient beings.

Dharma (dhamma):

The nature of existence, our destiny and the path of ultimate truth, ethics, right conduct and justice cosmic order and path of righteousness. The teachings of the Buddha which reflect the inherent goodness and universal ethical spiritual laws shared by all beings seeking the truth.

Eight Worldly Dharmas: (Vicissitudes)

The eight vicissitudes or pairs of opposites which one naturally encounters in the world of duality: Pleasure and pain; loss and gain; praise and blame; fame and disgrace (ill repute). A meditator endeavors to greet these energies with equanimity, wisdom, humor and innocent delight.

Emaho:
Marvelous

Hindrances:
The five mind energies that prevent one from seeing what is ultimately true and the classical obstacles to meditation: Craving; Aversion; Torpor; Restlessness ; Doubt

The Four Noble Truths:
The truth that suffering exists
The truth of the origin of suffering (craving and attachment)
The truth of the cessation of suffering
The truth of the means to the end of suffering (the noble eightfold path)

Karma:
The universal law of cause and effect. (We reap what we sow.) In the world of mind and matter, the intention of all thoughts, words and actions bear their own fruit in this lifetime or another, however subtle or profound they may seem.

Karuna: (one of the Brahma Viharas)
The compassion, empathy and affection that naturally arises out of a heart that does not cling and offers itself to all sentient beings without distinction. Compassion and gentle affection arising out of the the experience of oneness (wholeness/ emptiness).

Mala: (garland, rose)
A string of beads used to count the repetitions of a mantra (energy encapsulated in a mystical sound), similar to a rosary.

Mara:
A legendary mind demon and seductress of delusion. Also a symbol of the many destructive energies and forces, passions and desires that intoxicate us, hinder meditation, and tempt us away from the path of liberation.

Metta: (one of the Brahma Viharas)
Loving kindness, benevolence free of desire and equally aimed at all beings, friend, stranger and foe. The gentle friendliness and magnanimous feelings of unconditional caring that arise from an untainted heart and the direct knowledge that there is no separate self.

Metta Sutta:
Lovingkindess sutra (see pp. 218-219) to be read aloud to yourself and a friend.

Metta Ressolves:
The four lovingkindness phrases which cultivate a sense of connectedness and openhearted compassion for all beings in all realms, in all forms.
May I be free of danger.
May I have mental happiness.
May I have physical happiness.
May I have ease of well-being.

Mudita: (one of the Brahma Viharas)
Sympathetic joy and vicarious pleasure for the happiness of others. The true spirit of what is mine is yours, what is yours is mine. *Mudita* eradicates envy and a sense of aloneness.

Nirvana:
Enlightenment, the end of suffering, liberation from all earthly bondage and from *samsara* — the endless cycle of births and deaths.

   A state where one is empty of self and full of everythingness at the same time. The ultimate happiness that is all inclusive and yet empty of a differentiated self; and because it knows no separate self, it cannot adequately be described, as there is no one here to describe it.

Samadhi:
A high state of concentration or absorption. Fixing attention and firmly but gently establishing the mind's focus. The point at which the observer and the object of meditation (that which is observed) merge. (Step eight of the noble eightfold path.) In Hinduism *samadhi* = enlightenment.

Satori:
Enlightenment, the sudden and powerful experience of a moment of awakening.

Sila:
Moral conduct and humility arising from the experience of insight into the true nature of interdependence. Knowing no distinction between self-interest and the interest of others, one is inspired to live in a manner that is spacious and harmless.

Sangha:
The Buddhist community. An order of kindred spirits on a path of liberation.

The Eightfold Path:
The fourth noble truth and prescription for liberation.
Right Understanding
Right Thought
Right Speech
Right Action
Right Livelihood
Right Effort
Right Mindfulness
Right Concentration

Vipassana: (Vipashyana)
Insight, clear seeing, mindfulness practice. One sees the truth without delusion or the mind's distortion. Insight meditation, in the Buddhist tradition, gives insight into the nature of all experience. One is able to view the impermanence of all phenomena arsing and passing away with a perfect impartiality of mind, and a non-clinging heart.